Self-Publishing on KDP

KDP

A Step-by-Step Guide to using the Kindle Direct Publishing Website

Paul Gutiérrez Covey

CONTENTS

Self-Publishing on KDP

Introduction

Now more than ever, self-publishing has become quite popular. Before, aspiring authors had to write the manuscript, take it to a publisher, and pray that it would be accepted and published. This is a process that can take years; if you are lucky, it may take several months.

With publishing companies like Kindle Direct Publishing (KDP), however, you can publish a book in a matter of days. That is how quick and easy it is! The best part is that this process is completely free.

You do not have to pay anything up front, since this is a print-on-demand company. In other words, you do not have to worry about printing a large quantity of books, since Amazon will only print when books are ordered.

Being a free service, this may seem to be too good to be true. However, it does make sense. Being a free service, people will be more inclined to use it, and then, once the book is published, customers will purchase it, and that way, KDP will make money by taking a percentage off of the sales.

The only downside to this process is that you will have to do all the footwork yourself. While a traditional publisher will have the book formatted for you and will take care of the marketing, with self-publishing, that is all your job.

For some, this may be a deal-breaker. However, it does not need to be. Formatting the book does not have to be a complicated process, and marketing it can be done in a fairly simple way. KDP has all of the resources that you need to get the job done without having to spend a lot of money.

In this book, you will learn how to get your book published without paying a dime. You will learn to format the book, publish it, and market it. At the time of writing this book, I have already published five books, and so far the most I have spent on a book has been a dollar, and that is only because of what I wanted at the moment. You can do the same!

Keep in mind that there are many differences between an eBook and a Paperback, so most of the chapters will be divided in two. If you only want to publish one edition, you will need to look for the sections that deal with that particular edition type.

In case you are wondering, the two edition types that I mentioned are the only ones available on KDP right now. If you want a hardcover book or a cardboard book, you will need to do that on a different publishing platform.

DISCLAIMER

I would like to mention that regarding the formatting, the information found in this book will only work if you are using Microsoft Word. If you are using a Mac or any other type of computer that does not support this program, this advice may not be of much help to you.

Getting Started

Creating your account

So you want to publish a book, which is absolutely amazing! Congratulations for that, because it takes courage and skills to do that. Before anything, go ahead and create a KDP account. This is very simple, especially if you already have an Amazon account.

First off, you will need to go to kdp.amazon.com (do not add "www" at the beginning). You will see that there is a video of a guy at a computer, and to the right, you will see the "Sign in" button. If you already have an Amazon account, click on that. If not, click on the button underneath it that says "Sign up."

If you click "Sign in," just log in with your Amazon e-mail address and password. If you clicked "Sign up," you will see a log in screen. Click the "Create your KDP account" button at the bottom. Enter your name, then your e-mail, and then the password you want. You will need to re-enter the password on a second text box. Once you have entered the information, click "Create your KDP account."

Most likely, Amazon will send you an e-mail with a One Time Password (OTP). This is a six-digit number you will need to enter. Once you do, you will be able to start setting up your account.

Whether you clicked "Sign in" or "Sign up," you will see the Terms of Service. Read it and click the "Accept" button on the bottom-right. I know hardly anybody ever reads that, but it is always best to read the fine print.

Now you will be taken to your Bookshelf, which at the moment will be empty. At the very top, you will see an option that says "Your Account." Click on that, and it will ask you for a phone number. Enter a phone number that you have on hand, and choose whether you want a text message or a voice delivery (which is another way of saying a phone call).

Remember that if you are not located in the US, you will need to click on the US flag and choose the country where you are located. Once you have done that and your phone number is there, click on the "Send OTP" button. You will receive either a text message or a phone call (depending on which option you chose) with the six-digit number. Enter it in the text box and click "Ok."

You are now in your account information. To the left, you will see the account ID. This is very important because if you ever need to call KDP, they may need to ask you for that. You will also see a text box that asks you which country you are located in. Type in your country, and then select it, and more text boxes will appear.

Enter your information in the text boxes. In the "Name" section, do not enter a pseudonym; enter your real name. This information is not public, but if you do not enter your real name, there could be problems with the royalties later on.

Then, you will need to add your bank account information. First enter the country where your bank is located. Not all countries work for KDP bank information, so if you get a message saying that Electronic Funds Transfer is not available, you will need to settle for check payments or create a Payoneer account. There will be more information about that in the "Royalties" chapter of this book.

You are almost done now. The last step to get your account fully created is to take the tax interview. The information you enter here is required and handled by the IRS, so you do not have to worry about KDP taking your social security information. Do not contact

KDP to ask them what you should enter here, though. They do not handle this type of information, and they are not tax advisers. If you do not know what to enter, contact the IRS directly or a tax adviser, and they can provide better guidance.

Creating the Book

Now that your account is fully created, you can now focus on the publishing process. Of course, the first step in any publishing process is writing your manuscript. That part depends entirely on you. Once it is done, though, the next step is the formatting. Just know that KDP will not format your book for you. This is a do-it-yourself website, so any formatting, editorial, or any other services must be done outside of KDP.

For eBooks, formatting can be simple or complicated, depending on what you want to do. In most cases, though, it is very simple. Paperback formatting, however, can be just a little more complicated since you need to create a print-ready file.

In this chapter, you will learn everything you need to know in order to format both editions of your book. There is no need to hire a professional since with these tips, you will be able to make your book as professional as it gets!

Formatting your Paperback book

In most cases, professional book formatters use complicated programs like InDesign which are expensive and hard to use if you have not studied graphic designing. The good news is that you can format your Paperback book by using Microsoft Word, and it will still look just as professional.

In order to get this done, there are three methods you can choose from. You could download a template, use the Kindle Create add-in for Microsoft word, or you could do all the formatting yourself from scratch. I do not recommend the third option, since that could become quite tricky, so I will only explain the first two, since those options will ensure that your document will be perfect.

Now before we explore any of the formatting options, you will need to make one important decision, which is the trim-size. How big do you want your book to be? In most help pages on KDP, you will see that the most common trim-size is 6" x 9". Do not follow that advice blindly.

If you want to know which trim-size is best for you, grab a book that you like the size of and measure it. This book is a 5.5" x 8.5". In many cases, novels are 5" x 8". Ultimately, the decision is yours, but you should choose something you are comfortable with. Once you have made up your mind, you can begin the formatting process.

Templates

Using templates is by far the best and easiest option you can choose. In this case, everything is all formatted. You just need to insert the text. In order to download the templates, just visit kdp.amazon.com and click the "Help" option at the top-right. On the search bar, type in "Paperback Manuscript Templates" and press Enter. You do not need a KDP account to do this.

You will see a list of help pages, and the first one will show the name you just typed in. Click on it, and scroll down a little. You will see two download buttons. One is for blank templates, and the other is for templates with sample content. I recommend downloading both so that you can see which one works best for you.

If you use the blank template, you will have to design every single page. I recommend copying and pasting the chapters one by one. Whether you are using a blank template or not, copying and pasting entire chapters might affect the page size. A quick fix for that is to copy all but the very last period.

Be aware that when you add page numbers, you will need to add a section break. If not, page 1 will start on the first page right after the cover.

To get the right page numbers, go to the very last page before the first chapter starts and click the "Layout" tab at the top. You will see an option that says "Breaks." Click on that, and select the continuous break. Then, go to the first page of the first chapter and open the footer. You can do so by clicking on the "Insert" tab and choosing the "Footer" option.

Once you have the footer open, you will see the different options for that section at the top. The "Link to previous" option will be selected, so you will need to click it in order to de-select it. Once you have done that, Click "Page Numbers," and then "Page number formats." You must make sure that the "Start on" option is selected, and you should type in the number 1. Now you can click "Page Numbers" again and insert the page numbers there.

Table of Contents

To create a perfect Table of Contents, first you have to make sure that the chapter titles and subtitles are formatted correctly. You will need to select each chapter title and use the "Heading 1" option. At the top of Word, you will see the "Home" tab. Click on that, and on the right-hand side, you will see the styles. Click on "Heading 1," and your chapter title will change. Make sure it has the correct color and font you want it to have, and repeat this process on each of your chapters.

For sub-titles, there is the "Heading 2" option, and you will even find a "Heading 3" option if you need to. Make sure each of your chapter titles and subtitles have the correct headings, and you will be able to continue.

The next step is to go to the page where you want your Table of Contents. Select the "References" tab, and you will see the "Table of Contents" option on the left. Click it, and you will see the different options available. Select the one you like the most, and the Table of Contents will be generated automatically.

Adding images

If your book has images, adding them to a Paperback book is

fairly easy. Just insert the image where you want it, and resize it to look exactly the way you want it to look in the physical copy. Just remember, the way it looks in the file is exactly how it will look once it is printed. As long as the image is within the margins, you can put it anywhere you want and size it however you want.

The Kindle Create Add-in

If you want to format your book without the use of a template, you can use the Kindle Create Add-in for Microsoft Word. To download it, it is actually easier to find on Google than it is on the KDP site. Just search on Google for "Kindle Create Add-in," and you will see the following page: "Kindle Create Add-in for Microsoft Word (Beta) - Amazon KDP." Click on that, and then click the "Download now" button.

Once the add-in is downloaded, install it. Next time you open Microsoft Word, you will see a "Kindle" tab on the right. Now open your manuscript, and you will be able to start turning it into a perfectly formatted book.

With your manuscript open, start by clicking the "Kindle" tab at the top. To the left, you will see a button that says "Get Started." Click on that, and you will see an introduction window. Click "Continue" on bottom-right, and then you will be prompted to choose a theme. Select one, and click "Continue" once again.

The next step is to choose a trim size. At present, this add-in will only give two options, which are 6" x 9" and 8.5" x 11". Choose either one, and if you want to change it, you can do so. Just click the "Layout" tab and then click "Size." The last option will say "More Paper Sizes." Click on that, and you will be able to choose a custom size for your book.

The last step is to just click "Finalize" on the bottom right. Once that is done, you can now begin working on your book. On the "Kindle" tab, you will find a button that says "Insert Template Page." This is a fairly useful tool, since it will add a template page to wherever your cursor is.

Click on this button, and you will see that you can create a title page, a quote page, a dedication page, copyright page, and even a Table of Contents page. Do not select the Table of Contents page until the very end, though.

If you already have certain elements already made, live for example the cover page, you do not need to insert a template. Instead, you can use the "Apply Elements by Type" option. Select the text and click on that button on the "Kindle" tab. Select the options that best fit you, and you will transform the parts of that page to look the way you want them.

I recommend clicking on this button and exploring the different options. As a word of advice, though, do not use everything that is there just because it is there. If it works for you, use it. If it does not, then leave it alone.

Now for each of the chapters, there is another button that says "Apply Common Elements." Select each chapter name and click on that button, and then you should select the option that says "Chapter Title." If you have subtitles, select them and choose the "Chapter Subtitle" option.

Once all of the chapter titles and subtitles are formatted correctly, click on the "Prep for Publish" button, and select "Insert Page Numbers." You can also select the "Insert Headers" option if you want, which will add the book title and author name to the headers.

If you have any areas within the chapters that are separated (but not by any type of subtitle or anything like that), you can use the "Insert Separator" option. This will insert a small design that separates one section from another. The design of the separator will differ depending on the theme you chose at the beginning.

The information above shows the basics of what you can do. I recommend clicking on all the buttons there to see the many options you have, and that way you can add whatever elements suit your book the best. Once you are done, place your cursor where you want the Table of Contents to be, and click "Insert Template Page," and select "table of contents page." As long as you followed all of the instructions above, a Table of Contents will be created.

The correct format for your Paperback book

No matter which method you used to create the book, you will need to save it in the correct format. You can upload the Word document if you want; however, the system will automatically convert it to PDF, and in that automatic conversion, your file could be changed different ways.

To avoid this, it is always best to save your manuscript as a PDF before uploading it. To do that, click on "File" on the top-left corner, and click "Save as." Click "Browse," and the "Save as" window will show up. On the bottom, you will see a drop-down menu that says "Save as type." Click on that menu and choose the PDF option. You can now save your file.

Paperback Cover

Once your manuscript is fully formatted, it is time to work on a cover. If you do not want to pay a designer, you have two options: you can create a PDF cover, or you can use the Cover Creator.

Cover Creator

The Cover Creator is a free tool that KDP offers for you to be able create a cover without too much hassle. You do not need to know anything about dimensions nor margins, since almost everything will be done for you.

When you are creating your book on KDP, you will find a section for uploading files. In another chapter you will learn all about the process of setting the book up on KDP, but for now I will only focus on this section.

Near the bottom, you will see a section that says "Book Cover," and there will be a button that says "Launch Cover Creator." Click on that and wait a minute for the tool the load. You will then see a window for choosing the main image. You can use one of KDPs stock images by selecting the "From Image Gallery" option, or you can upload your own by selecting the "From My Computer" option. If you want, you can also skip this step.

Next, you will see the different designs that are available. Some will allow you to add text on the front cover while others require the image to already have the text. Choose whichever one you like the best, and if you change your mid later, you will be able to change it at any time.

To tell the difference of which allow you to add text, you will see that some have the title of your book on them in a generic font. Those allow for text on the front cover. Once you have made up your mind, click on the design that you want.

Depending on which design you chose, you might have the option to upload a back cover image. You will know because the back cover will have an orange triangle at the top-left corner, and when you hover the mouse over it, it will say "Click to Edit or Change Image." Click on that, and you will be able to choose a second image by following the same process as the first one.

If you do not like the design that you chose, click on the "Choose Design" option on the top-left corner. You will then be taken back to the previous section. Choose the design you want and repeat until you are completely satisfied.

Below the cover, you will see three buttons: a paintbrush, a layout, and a text-box. The first one is to choose the color scheme. Click on it, and you can either select a preset color scheme, or you can choose custom colors.

The layout button is to choose the structure of the cover. Click on it, and you will see the different layouts you can choose from. You can click on each of them to preview them, and then click on the layout button again once you have decided.

Finally, the text-box button will allow you to change the fonts of the text. You were probably thinking that it would allow you to add text boxes (that is what I thought the first time I saw it). However, all the possible text-boxes are already there. I highly recommend using this option. Choose the font you like the most.

Once your cover looks exactly how you want it to, you can start adding text. Click anywhere where you see text, and you will be able to edit it. There should also be a section for the author picture. Click on that, and upload a good picture of yourself (or the author you are publishing for).

Finally, you will need to click on the "Preview" button at the bottom of the screen. You will then see a preview of how your cover will look. If you are satisfied, click "Save & Submit." If not, click "Style & Edit" on the top-left and make the necessary changes.

Print-Ready PDF Cover

If you want to upload your own PDF cover, you can certainly do so. For that, you can use programs like PowerPoint, Word, Illustrator, or websites like Canva or Adobe Spark. What you need to know, though, are the dimensions.

In order to figure out how big your file should be, you first need to have your manuscript fully formatted, because you need to know how many pages it will have. Once you know that, go to kdp.amazon.com and click on the "Help" option on the top-right.

In the text-box, type in "Paperback Cover Resources" and press Enter. Click on the help page with the name you typed in, and you will see a video. Under that, you will see three bullet points. The third one says "Try our calculator" at the end. Click on that, and then you will see two buttons that say "Download Calculator." Click on the first one and download the file.

The file you will download will be an Excel file. Open it, and click "Enable Content" at the top. You will now need to select the "Ink & Paper Choice." Whichever option you choose here should be the same one you choose when you create the book. Next, select the trim size, and enter the number of pages.

Make sure that all the information you entered is correct, and then click the "Cover" button. You will then see a template of a cover, and below it, you will see three numbers. The third one (and biggest) is the full width. On the right, you will see another three numbers. Again, the third one (and biggest) is the full height.

On the left, you will see more numbers. This is just to know how big the spine is, but you do not need to add that to the width, since as I mentioned, the full width already shows below. The first number there is a spine width.

The width and height are what you will need to size the document that you create for the cover, no matter which program or website you are using. Once you have sized it correctly, you can start designing your cover.

If you want some additional guidance, you can download a template as well. On the "Help" section of KDP, type in "Paperback Cover Resources" once again, and right above the "Try our calculator" option, you will see another option that says "Download one of our templates." Click on that link, and you will need to enter the trim-size of your book, the page count, and the page color.

Click "Download Cover Template," and a zip file will be downloaded. Unzip it, and you will find a PNG file and a PDF. For most programs, the PDF will not be useful since most programs are unable to edit it.

This template will show you exactly where all the margins are and the safe zones. You can delete the template from the design when you are done creating it.

Save your file as a PDF, and you will be able to upload it. For most programs, you will be able to just click on the "Save as" button as explained with the interior file, and you can save it as a PDF.

Formatting your eBook

As I mentioned above, formatting an eBook can be fairly simple. If what you want is a normal eBook that just flows smoothly (which is the most recommended), all you need to do is to create a Word document.

Some people pay to have an ePub file made, but that is not at all necessary; it is just a waste of money, since a Word file can be uploaded, and it can look just as professional as any other eBook you may find. When using Word, there are several aspects you must keep in mind, which I will detail ahead.

Page Breaks

First, you need to make sure that every chapter is separated by a page break. It is a common practice to just press the Enter key as many times as needed to get from one page to another, but that will not work for an eBook.

When you upload your document, it will be converted to eBook format. Since it is flowable (in other words, it does not have specific pages like a Word document does), the sections where you pressed Enter many times will not look the way you are expecting; it will certainly look off. By inserting a page break, though, it will be perfectly fine.

You can insert a page break in two different ways. The easiest method is to press Ctrl + Enter. By pressing these two buttons at the same time, you will automatically be on the next page. If you are not fond of keyboard combinations, click the "Insert" tab at the top of Word, and on the left, you will see an option that says "Page Break." Clicking on that will have the same effect.

Table of Contents

Now that the chapters are divided correctly, it is time to make a Table of Contents. Part of the information here will be identical to what you read for the paperback, but read anyway, since there are some differences.

For eBooks, you do not need page numbers; depending on the size and settings of each device or app, different people will see the pages in a different way. While one person may have a book with 150 pages, another person may have the same book with 215 pages.

Since there are no page numbers, you may wonder why you

would need a Table of Contents. The reason is twofold: on one hand, it tells the readers how many chapters there are, and on the other hand, if you create it right, readers will be able to touch a chapter name, and they will be taken directly to that chapter.

To create a perfect Table of Contents, first you have to make sure that the chapter titles and subtitles are formatted correctly. You will need to select each chapter title and use the "Heading 1" option. At the top of Word, you will see the "Home" tab. Click on that, and on the right-hand side, you will see the styles. Click on "Heading 1," and your chapter title will change. Make sure it has the correct color and font you want it to have, and repeat this process on each of your chapters.

For sub-titles, there is the "Heading 2" option, and you will even find a "Heading 3" option if you need to. Make sure each of your chapter titles and subtitles have the correct headings, and you will be able to continue.

The next step is to go to the page where you want your Table of Contents. Select the "References" tab, and you will see the "Table of Contents" option on the left. Click it, and you will see the different options available. Select the one you like the most, and the Table of Contents will be generated automatically.

Adding images

If your book has images, this could get a bit trickier. You may be tempted to add an image on the side and allow the text to continue next to it; however, this cannot be done. To add an image, you must first make sure to add it on a separate line. In other words, right after the text where you want to place it, press Enter and insert the image.

Now that the image is on your document, resize it in a way that the sides reach both margins. Then press Enter again where you want the text to continue. If you want the images to show in a different way, like for example with text next to them, you will need to read ahead and see how to use Kindle Create.

Using Kindle Create

If you want a print-replica eBook, or if you want a book with many images or even a comic book, a simple Word document will not be enough. Instead, you will need to use Kindle Create. Do not confuse it with the Kindle Create Add-in which is for Word; this is a free program that KDP offers in order to format your eBook. Be aware, though, that if you upload a file generated by this program, you will not be able to use any other file type for that book in the future.

The first step, of course, is to download and install the program. For that, just visit kdp.amazon.com and click the "Help" option at the top-right. On the search bar, type in "Getting Started with Kindle Create," and press Enter, and among the search results, the first one should be the help page with the name you just typed in.

Click on that help page, and you will see the options to download the program. Click on the download button, and once it has been downloaded, install it. Now that you have the program, the best course of action is to create a PDF file with your manuscript. If you create a Paperback edition, you can use that same file. If you did not, please go back to the Paperback formatting section and follow the instructions there to create your file.

With your PDF file ready, it is time to launch Kindle Create. Click on the "New Project From File" button, and on the left you will see two options for file types. The first one says "Novels, Essays, Poetry, Narrative Non-fiction." This option, in my opinion, is totally unnecessary, since you will get the same results by uploading a Word document to KDP.

The second option you will see says "Textbooks, Travel Guides, Cookbooks, Music books." Click on this option, and on the right, click "Choose File." Search for your file and double click it, and the file will load onto the program. When it shows up, review it, and once you are satisfied, click the "Save" option on the top-right.

After saving your book, you will need to click the "Publish" button, also on the top-right. This will export your file to KPF, which is an eBook format. Choose where you want to save the KPF file, and click "Save." You are now ready to upload your file.

EBook Cover

As with the Paperback, you also have two options to create your cover for the eBook, which is the Cover Creator and an image file. The difference is that an eBook does not require a back cover nor spine. Also, since dimensions are not such a big issue, you do not have to worry about it being exact like with the Paperback cover.

Cover Creator

The Cover Creator is much like the one for the Paperback, although not identical. If you want identical covers, this is not the best option for you.

If you already read the section about the Paperback Cover Creator, than you can skip this section. It only exists for those who only want to create a Kindle edition and do not want to create a Paperback.

If you choose to use the Cover Creator, on the contents page of the eBook on KDP, click on the "Launch Cover Creator" button. You will see a window that says "How to Use Cover Creator." Since you are reading this, you will not need that.

Click "Continue," and you will see a window for selecting an image. You can choose to select an image from the gallery, upload your own image, our you can just skip that step altogether. After you have selected the image, choose a design. All of the designs have the option to add text, so if your image already has text, you do not need the Cover Creator.

Select a design, and you will be able to start working on the cover. If later on you change your mind, you can change the design at any time. Just click the "Choose Design" option on the top-left corner, and you will be able to select a different design

At the bottom, you will see three buttons: a paintbrush, a layout, and a text-box. The first one is to choose the color scheme. Click on it, and you can either select a preset color scheme, or you can choose custom colors.

The layout button is to choose the structure of the cover. Click on it, and you will see the different layouts you can choose from. You can click on each of them to preview them, and then click on the layout button again once you have decided.

Finally, the text-box button will allow you to change the fonts of the text. Choose the style you like the best, and the fonts will be changed. I highly recommend using this option, since the default font does not look the greatest.

Once your cover looks exactly how you want it to, you can start editing any text that you want to edit. Click anywhere where you see text, and you will be able to edit it.

Finally, you will need to click on the "Preview" button at the bottom of the screen. You will then see a preview of how your cover will look. If you are satisfied, click "Save & Submit." If not, click "Style & Edit" on the top-left and make the necessary changes.

Uploading a JPEG image

There is not really much to say here, since you do not have to worry about dimensions in the same way you do about Paperback books. You can use websites like Canva and Adobe Spark to create a cover image, save it as a PDF, and then upload it to KDP. If you do not know how to do any of this, you are better off using the Cover Creator instead.

Creating your Book on KDP

With your files fully formatted, you can create the book on the website. It is not just a matter of uploading files; you will need to enter all of the metadata (information associated to the book), like the title name, author name, ISBN, etc.. In this section, you will learn exactly how you can create your book on the KDP website.

First of all, you will need to go to KDP and sign in. If you are already there, make sure you are on your bookshelf. No matter which KDP page you may be on, you should see the "Bookshelf" option at the top.

On the bookshelf, you will see a section that says "Create a New Title." Under that are the "Kindle eBook" and Paperback" options. You will need to start with one, so choose the one you want to work on first. Once you have set one up, the book will show up on the bottom of the bookshelf.

If you decided to work on the eBook first, below it you will see the option to "Create Paperback." If you decided to create the Paperback first, above it, you will see the "Create Kindle eBook" option instead.

Once you have selected either of the two, you will have to enter the metadata. Ahead, you will see each of the items that you must enter. Some only apply to eBooks while others only apply to Paperbacks.

Details

When creating a book on KDP, you will find three different pages. The first one is the "Details" page. Here you will be able to enter most of the metadata. For Paperbacks, be very careful what you enter, because once the book is live, most of these items cannot be changed. There will be more information about that further ahead, though.

Language

The first item you will find is the language. This is fairly simple; which language did you write your book in? That is what you will have to select. If the language is not in this drop-down menu, though, you will not be able to publish your book on KDP. For a list of supported languages, you can search the "Help" section for a page called "Supported Languages."

Interestingly, there are some languages that are only supported for eBooks. For example, if you wrote your book in Tamil, you will be able to publish an eBook edition, but not a Paperback.

The next section is the "Book Title." This includes title and subtitle. If you are publishing both editions, make sure the names match exactly, because if not, your editions will not link on Amazon, and no agent will link them for you.

Series

Next comes the series information. This is optional; if your book is not part of a series, you can leave this blank. If it is, then you will need to include the series title and the volume number. The series name should be identical for all books in the series if you want them to be part of a series bundle.

When entering the series number, you must add a natural number, and not a roman numeral. For the books to be part of a series bundle, make sure that you do not include decimal numbers nor the number zero.

Edition Number

After the series information, you will find the edition number. Again, this is optional. Normally, second edition of a book will have a different ISBN, so if you are publishing a book and then later on you want to make edits to the manuscript, do not think you will be able to change the edition number to the already-published book. For that, you would need to publish a new book with a different ISBN, and then you could enter edition number 2.

Author & Contributors

You will then find the "Author" and "Contributors" sections. You can add up to ten authors and contributors. For Paperbacks, you will see text boxes to enter the prefix, first name, middle name, last name, and suffix. Do not fill in a box just because it is there; only enter it if you want it to show up on Amazon on the author name.

For eBook, you will only see first name and last name. If you want a middle initial, you will need to add it in the "First name" text box. You can add all of the same information, except that you do not have all of the text boxes like with the Paperback.

Description

The following section is for the description. What you write here is what will show up on Amazon as the description. It will not automatically show up on the back-cover, as some may think; it only affects the Amazon detail page.

When entering a description on an eBook, you can press enter to create paragraph breaks however you want, and it will look just the way you want it to. However, on the Paperback, it will not work that way. Once you publish it, it will look like one long paragraph.

To create several paragraphs, you will need to use HTML. For paragraph breaks (in which there is a space between each paragraph), you will need to add <p> at the beginning of every paragraph and </p> at the end. If you only want a line break (in other words, no spaces between paragraphs), just add <br> at the end of every paragraph without adding any other HTML tag.

There are other HTML tags you can use as well. For example, for bold words, add <b> at the beginning of the bold text and </b> at the end. For italic, add <i>> at the beginning of the italic text and </i> at the end. For a list of HTML tags you can use, search the "Help" section for a page called "Supported HTML for Book Description." These tags can be used for eBooks as well if that is what you want to do.

Publishing Rights

The next it is the Publishing Rights; indicate whether you own the copyright or if the book is Public Domain. This can be a bit confusing sometimes, but the first thing you need to know is that by US law, if you publish a book, it is automatically protected by copyright. If you want to pay the copyright branch of the government for additional protection, that is fine, and it will be perfect if there is any type of legal dispute in the future.

Public Domain refers to any book that nobody holds the copyright to anymore. For example, since Bram Stoker passed away so long ago, "Dracula" would be considered a Public Domain book. If you just wrote your book this year, it is certainly not within this classification, so do not select it.

If you want to pay for copyright for additional protection, that is up to you; KDP will not do this for you. You will need to look for the copyright branch of the government of the country where you are located for this.

Keywords

After the publishing rights, you will see a section for keywords. These can be words or phrases that customers could enter and find your book. Do not think, though, that whatever you enter here will guarantee that customers will find your book if they type that in. If there are many other items on Amazon with the same keyword and with more relevance, your book may not be found.

Whatever you type here, make sure it is not already in the description nor the title, since anything in those sections are already keywords in the system. Write other words or phrases that are related to your book. If you cannot think of anything, you can just leave this section blank, since it is optional.

Categories

Now it is time to choose categories for your book. On this section, you can choose two. However, once the book is published, you can request more. There will be more information about that later on in this book.

What you must keep in mind when choosing these categories is that what you see here is not exactly how it will show up on Amazon. You may be wondering why, and there is a logical explanation for this. You see, on the different Amazon marketplaces, the categories are different, so if KDP were to put exact categories just the way they show up on Amazon, it would be a mess. So the categories here are more generic, and they determine what the categories will be on each of the Amazon marketplaces where the book will be made live.

For now, just add the two categories that fit your book the most. Once it becomes live, you will be able to see exactly how the category will look on each marketplace, and you can decide what actions to take from there.

Once the book is live, you will be able to ask for up to ten categories to be assigned to your book, so do not think that you are only limited to the two categories in this section.

Age and Grade Range

If what you are working on is an eBook, the next two sections you will see are "Age and Grade Range" and "Pre-Order." Paperbacks do not have these sections. For the "Age and Grade Range" section, choosing the ranges is optional. However, if your book is for children or for teens and young adults, you will need to choose an age range if you want categories for the specific age ranges. If not, you can skip it.

The grade range is mostly for academic books. Again, this section is optional, so if your book does not have to do at all with school, there is no need to select any of the options.

Pre-Orders

As mentioned above, Pre-Orders are only for eBooks. If you want to create a pre-order for a Paperback, you can create an Amazon Advantage account and create the pre-order listing there. Once the book becomes live with KDP, you will have to fulfill any pre-orders yourself, though, since KDP will not do it for you.

For eBooks, you can set a pre-order for a whole year in the future. Keep in mind, though, that if you cancel the pre-order once it is on Amazon, you will be penalized for a whole year of not being able to create pre-orders.

Once the pre-order is live on Amazon, you can move the date ahead of time if you are ready sooner, or you can delay it once by one month if you need more time. After that, you can delay it a second time, but you will be penalized in the same way as when cancelling a pre-order.

Adult Content

For Paperbacks, the last section on the details page is "Adult Content." EBooks do not have this section, so you will only see it on the Paperbacks. Only select "Yes" if your book is erotica or has any type of content that is not at all suitable for a child to read.

Sometimes people select the "Yes" option because they say that the book is for adults and not for children, but that is not how it works. If you select "Yes," your book will not show up in any Amazon search results, because Amazon wants to make sure that a child will not accidentally find your book and buy it.

Content

Once you have finished with the "Details" section, click the "Save and Continue" button at the bottom, and you will be directed to the "Contents" section. This page deals mostly with the files, but there are some additional items to look at as well. The items are different for both editions, so they will be explained separately.

Paperback Content

Print ISBN

All Paperback books must have an ISBN. You can either request a free KDP ISBN, or you can purchase one from Bowker. An ISBN is not cheap though; just one can cost around $125. Now there are several aspects to take into account for both options here.

If you choose a free KDP ISBN, as the name implies, you will not have to pay anything for it. However, the publisher will show up on Amazon as "Independently Published." Nobody has the power to change that, so do not even bother contacting KDP to request for them to change it.

Another aspect about this ISBN is that you will not be able to use it anywhere else. Now be careful with this; some people misinterpret this and think that you will not be able to publish your book anywhere else, which is not true. The book is yours, so you own the copyright. An ISBN has absolutely nothing to do with the copyright of the book.

If you want to publish your book on another self-publishing

website, you can do so. However, if you used a free KDP ISBN, you will need to use a different ISBN on the other website. For most people, this is not a big deal. Nonetheless, this can cause confusion with the readers, since the same book will be found with two different ISBNs without them being different types of editions.

If you purchase your own ISBN from Bowker, you can enter it into this section on KDP, and you will also be asked for the imprint name. The imprint name is the same as the publisher name that you entered in Bowker. Do not make the mistake of typing the word "Bowker" here.

Moreover, when you purchase the ISBN, you will be asked to register the title, subtitle, publisher name, etc.; you will need to add all of the information about the book. When entering this information to KDP, you will need to add it exactly how your registered it on Bowker, because if not, the KDP system will detect a mismatch.

If after registering the information to the ISBN you decide you want to change something, you may have to wait around a week for KDPs system to detect the change. Because of this, it is best to make sure that you add all of the information correctly from the very beginning.

Publication Date

The publication date is the next item on the list. This is only for books that were already published before, so you can enter the date that the book was first published. If the book was never published before, just leave this blank, and the publication date will be added automatically the day it goes live.

It is common to make the mistake of thinking a future date can be added here to create a pre-order, or to set the date that you want the book to go live. This is not actually possible; the only way to determine when it goes live is by actually publishing it at the time you want it live.

Print Options

The print options are of utmost importance, because they determine exactly how your book will look once it is printed. First, you will choose the interior and paper type. If you choose color, keep in mind that it does not matter how many pages actually have color; the whole book will be considered full color. The reason behind this is the fact that it will all be printed on one printer with the color setting on it. This will not affect the cover, though, since covers are always printed on color printers.

Full color books will always be printed on white paper. If your book will be black & white, then you can choose between cream or white paper. Most of the time, fictional books are printed with cream paper, and non-fictions are printed with white paper. However, the choice is ultimately yours.

Then you can choose the trim size. If you want to ever get your book into a bookstore, it would be best to choose a standard trim size. However, you can also choose a custom one if you want. There are limits, though. For the width, you can choose anywhere between 4" and 8.5", and for the height, you can choose anywhere between 6" and 11.69". Anything outside of those ranges is not possible.

Bleed is for books that have images that go outside of the margins. For example, if your book has an image that covers the whole page, and there is no white border around it, you will need bleed.

Before selecting this option, make sure that you add an eighth of an inch more to each outer margin of your book. For example, for a 5" x 8" book, the file should actually be 5.125" x 8.25". Otherwise, the book will not meet the requirements.

The last print option is the cover finish. Matte covers are leathery, while the Glossy covers are laminated. If you are not sure which one to choose, order a proof copy of one first, and then order a proof copy of the other. There will be more information ahead about ordering proof copies.

Regarding the different print options, it is important to know that the only one that will affect the printing costs of the book is the interior type. A full color book is more expensive to print than a black & white book. The number of pages will also affect the price. None of the other options actually matter.

Manuscript and Book Cover

The next step is to upload your files. Click on the "Upload paperback manuscript" button, and find your manuscript file. It will then take a few seconds to upload the file, and after that, you can proceed to the cover section.

On the "Book Cover" section, you will see the Cover Creator option by default. If you want to use this tool, click on the "Launch Cover Creator" button and create your cover. If you already have a PDF file, below you will see an option that says "Upload a cover you already have." Click on that, and you will be able to upload your file.

If your cover has a barcode, click on the checkbox below indicating that it already has one before you upload it. If it does not have a barcode, leave the checkbox unchecked. With that out of the way, click on the "Upload your cover file" button and select your cover file.

Book Preview

The final step on this page is to preview your book. This step is mandatory, and if you ever make any little change on the "Contents" section, you will need to preview the book again. Click on the "Launch Previewer" button, and you may have to wait a few minutes or even longer, depending on the size of your files.

While waiting for the previewer to launch, you may see some messages saying to go grab a sandwich or something like that. It is just part of the sense of humor programed into the system. Once it has loaded, you will see the cover of your book. Move the arrow onto the cover, and you will see some arrow buttons. Click on them to look through your book.

On the left, if there are any errors, you will see the word "Errors" in red letters. If it is there, you will also see the page numbers, so you can click on them to see where the errors are exactly. They will be highlighted on the pages. Make sure to fix the errors on the file, re-upload it, and then launch the previewer again. Once there are no errors and you are satisfied, click the "Approve" button.

EBook Content

Manuscript

On the "Manuscript" section for eBooks, you will see two different parts: Digital Rights Management (DRM) and the upload button. Choose well whether you want DRM or not, because once your eBook is live, you will not be able to change this.

DRM is basically a way in which you can protect your work from piracy. Basically, it does not allow readers to copy any parts of the manuscript. If you have a reference book that is meant to be quoted, this might not be a good thing, but for other books, you may want to consider it.

There is much debate as to how good DRM is for you, but in the end, it is up to you whether you want to enable it or not. Since this is a free website, you do not have to pay anything extra for this.

Choose whether you want DRM or not, and then upload your manuscript. The process is simple; just click the "Upload eBook manuscript" button and select your file.

Kindle eBook Cover

Now it is time to upload your cover. Just like with the Paperback, you can either use the Cover Creator, or you can upload a cover that you already have. To use the Cover Creator, just click the "Launch Cover Creator" button, and you will be able to create your cover online using this tool.

If you already have a cover, just click on the option below that says "Upload a cover you already have." Your best bet will be to upload a JPG file; you can upload a TIFF, but JPG files are much easier to work with.

Kindle eBook Previewer

Unlike with the Paperback, the previewer is not mandatory for the eBook. You can skip it if you want, but it is not recommendable to do so. If you want to preview your book, click "Launch Previewer," and you will be able to see exactly how your eBook will look on different devices.

If you want, you can also download your file. If you uploaded files that are fully formatted as eBooks, most likely the system will not allow you to download it, though. If you are able to, you click either "Preview on your Computer" or "Preview on your Kindle Device." Either option will give you the download links.

You can download a special previewer if you want, and below those options, you will see the links to download either HTML or MOBI. Download the MOBI if you want to preview it on a Kindle device or app.

Kindle eBook ISBN

For eBooks, an ISBN is not necessary, and adding one will make absolutely no difference at all, so in reality, it is almost a waste of money to add one. If you still want to, though, you can go ahead and add your ISBN here.

Below the ISBN section, you will see a place to enter the publisher. You can enter this even if you do not have an ISBN, so as to make it look more professional.

Keep in mind that even if you add an ISBN to your eBook, it will not show up on the Amazon detail page of your book. If you add a publisher name, though, it will show up for everyone to see. If you do not add a publisher name, the default is "Amazon Digital Services LLC." You decide whether you want that name or not.

Rights and Pricing

Once you have finished with the "Content" section, click the "Save and Continue" button at the bottom, and you will be taken to the "Rights and Pricing" page, which is the last page you will have to fill out before publishing your book.

Just like with the "Content" page, "Rights and Pricing" differs between Paperback and eBook. Both editions need different types of settings, so again, you will see the explanation of both types separately so that it can be clearer to you.

Paperback Rights and Pricing

Territories

The first setting to configure is "Territories." Basically, where do you want your book to be sold. Unless your book is Public Domain only in specific places, or you have some type of contract that only allows you to sell in certain countries, you may want to select the "All Territories" option. Sometimes authors do not want to sell in all countries, but that only limits the number of people who can buy your book.

If for some reason you do want to limit the countries where your book will be sold, select the "Individual Territories" option, and make sure that only the countries you want to sell in are selected. You must have at least one selected; you cannot publish a book without making it live on Amazon.

Pricing & Royalty

This may be one of the most important parts of all; the price that your book will sell for. There is a text box where you can enter the price you want, and below that, you will see the minimum list price. Since this whole process is totally free, there has to be a minimum list price that will guarantee that Amazon will make a profit. If you set the same price as the minimum, though, you will not make any money at all, so you will need to set something higher. If you select Expanded Distribution, the minimum list price will be higher to account for the difference in royalties.

Now the way the royalties works is that you receive 60% of the list price minus printing costs for any sale on Amazon. Once you enter a price, you will see the printing costs to the right and the royalties you will receive.

Expanded Distribution royalties are different. Before explaining that, it is best that you understand what this is. If you enroll your book into Expanded Distribution, it will be placed on the Ingram catalog (www.ingramcontent.com). There, bookstores and online retailers will be able to purchase your book at a wholesale price.

Since your book would be sold at a lower price, your royalties for any of these sales would be lower. Any time a bookstore or an online retailer purchases your book, you will receive 40% minus printing costs. You will see the royalties for Expanded distribution below the one for Amazon.

Below, you will see an option that says "7 other marketplaces." Click on that, and you can manually select the prices for the other marketplaces where your book will be for sale. If you want the price to be the same everywhere, you can skip this step.

Request a Printed Proof

Before you publish your book, it is recommendable that you purchase a printed proof. You may have previewed the book digitally, but what you see on a monitor and what is actually printed are two very different things.

To order a proof, click the option at the bottom that says "Request printed proofs of this book." You will be able to order up to five. Select the quantity, and then select a marketplace. The marketplace of the order determines the country where it will be printed, so for the US, you would select Amazon.com.

Once you have selected the quantity and marketplace, click

"Submit Proof Request." A pop-up window will appear letting you know that it can take up to four hours to process your request, and that you will receive an e-mail once it is done. Click "Confirm Proof Request" and wait.

Within four hours, you will receive an e-mail letting you know that the proof is ready, and you will see a link where you can order it. Clicking on that link will take you to your Amazon shopping cart or basket. Place the order like you would with any other Amazon order. Since this is from KDP and not Amazon, Prime will not work, so do not expect free shipping.

Once you receive your proof, you will see a band on it that says "Not for Resale," and on the back, you will see a barcode that does not match the one that should be on your book. This is totally normal; all proof copies are like that. The final version will not have this band, nor will it have the barcode that the proof copy has.

KDP Select Enrollment

For eBooks, the first section you will find is "KDP Select." This is an exclusivity program that applies only to eBooks. If you enroll, you are agreeing that you will only sell the eBook with KDP. You can still publish and sell the Paperback edition anywhere else, since this program only affects eBooks.

The good news is that you can change this setting at any time. If you enroll and later on want to sell the book somewhere else, just contact KDP support and request for your book to be removed from this program.

There are three benefits to enrolling your book into KDP Select, which are free book promotions, Countdown Deals, and Kindle Unlimited. Some may not consider these benefits, but that depends on what you want for your book.

Every 90 days, you have the right to create either a free book promotion or a Countdown Deal. A free book promotion, as the name implies, is a promotion in which your book will be free for up to five days (you choose the number of days). Of course, you will not receive any royalties for any sales made for this book while it is free; this is mostly to gain visibility and an audience.

Countdown Deals are discounts in which your book will have a lower price, and there will be a timer showing exactly how long the price will be there. You can set increments so that the price will gradually go up until it is back to the regular price.

Finally, we have the Kindle Unlimited advantage. Any customer who has a Kindle Unlimited membership will be able to read your book for free if it is enrolled in KDP Select. You will be paid per page read. There is no exact amount that you would be paid, since it depends on how much money is made with Kindle Unlimited, but I can tell you that it is a very low amount. The advantage is that more people may read your book, increasing the chances of receiving a customer review.

Territories

Just as with the Paperback, you will be able to select the territories where you want your book to be sold. You can either select "All Territories" or "Individual Territories." That way you can have control over where your book is sold and where it will not be available for purchase.

Royalty and Pricing

After selecting the territories, you will be able to set the price of your eBook. If you want, you can click the button that says "View Service" under "KDP Pricing Support (Beta)," and you can see some ideas for prices. This is not eligible for all categories, though.

Below the price text box, you will see a minimum list price; you will not be able to set your book for free, though, so do not even think about that. The lowest price you can set is $0.99.

There are two different royalty plans you can choose from, and the price you can set depends on which plan you choose. For the 35% plan, you will get exactly 35% of the list price, and you can set any price you want between $0.99 and $200 (as long as the file is not too big). If the file size is high, the minimum price may go up, which is why it is recommendable to upload a simple Word document.

If you want the 70% royalty plan, you are limited to setting your price anywhere between $2.99 and $9.99. With this plan, you will receive 70% of the list price minus delivery cost, which is a fee depending on how big the file is. In most cases, this fee is not even a dollar, but the bigger the file is, the higher the delivery cost goes.

Below the main price, you can click the "Other marketplaces (12)" option in order to manually set prices in other countries. Keep in mind that no matter which price you set in another country, you will always see the price of your home marketplace for digital content. This is normal, and not a sign of a price error.

Book Lending

The next section you will see is "Book Lending." This will allow readers to lend the books to other readers for a 14-day period. If you chose the 70% royalty plan, it will be activated, though, and you will not have the option to deactivate it.

Publishing your Book

Now that you have finished entering all of the information, you can now publish the book. On the bottom right, will see a button that says "Publish you Paperback Book" or "Publish your Kindle eBook." Click that button, and your book will be submitted for review. If it meets all of the requirements, it will go live on Amazon.

Keep in mind that for the Paperback, if you requested a proof copy, it does not matter how good it looks; if it does not meet the requirements, it will not go through. You may contact KDP and complain and say that it is good enough for you, but it will not matter, since it will not be accepted until all requirements are met.

Once the book is live, you must take into consideration that there are items that cannot be changed. For eBooks, you can change almost everything; the only thing you cannot change is the DRM setting. However, for Paperback books, most items are locked, and you will not be able to change them no matter how much you ask them to do it. Ahead you will see a full list of items that you will not be able to change on a Paperback once it has been published:

> Title
> Subtitle
> Primary author name
> ISBN
> Trim size
> Imprint name
> Ink & paper type
> Language
> Edition
> Publication date

If you have already published your Paperback and you realize that one or more of these items have errors, then you will need to unpublish the book and publish a new edition with a new ISBN. If the book has not had any sales, you could even request for the Amazon detail page to be removed. If even one customer has purchased a copy, though, KDP will not remove it.

Unpublishing your Book

If at any time you want to unpublish your book, you can certainly do so at any time. On your KDP Bookshelf, go to the far right of the book, and you will see a small button with three dots (…). Hover you cursor over that button, and a menu will appear. At the bottom, you will see an option that either says "Unpublish eBook" or "Unpublish Print Book." Click on that option, and a pop-up window will appear where you can just click the "Unpublish" button.

When you unpublish a book, this will not remove the Amazon detail page; the book will still be on Amazon, but it will show as unavailable. For the Paperback edition, if there are any copies in the warehouse, the book will remain for sale until the copies are sold.

Now you are probably thinking that it is impossible for there to be copies in stock since KDP is print on demand; however, although that is true, it is possible. If a customer returns a book in perfect condition, or if a customer places an order but cancels it after it is printed, there will be physical stock.

Moreover, if there are any third-party sellers who are selling the book, they have the right to do so. If they own a printed copy of the book, they can sell it in the same way you can resell a book you purchased at a local bookstore.

Royalties and Sales Reports

With your book published, you will now be expecting to receive money for your sales, and you will want to be able to track any movements. This chapter will explain everything you need to know about getting paid for your books and checking the reports.

Whenever you make any sales, you will be paid at the end of the second month after the sale was made. In other words, any books sold in January will be paid at the end of March. As long as your selling every month, you will be paid every month, but the first time you will have to wait.

Sales Dashboard

If you want to find out how many people are buying your book, you will need to check the sales reports. On any KDP page, you will see several options at the top; the first one is "Bookshelf," and next to it is "Reports." Click on "Reports," and you will be taken to your Sales Dashboard.

On this page, you will see several reports tabs, some filtering options, and then two graphs. If you see any vertical lines on the graphs, that means you have had sales. They are color coded, so hover your cursor over any of the lines and you will see exactly what type of book was sold.

The second graph you will see is for the number of pages read on Kindle Unlimited and Kindle Owners' Lending Library, which applies only if your book is enrolled into KDP Select. Below this graph, you will see the exact number of royalties earned in the last 90-day period.

Something important to keep in mind is that since this is only a 90-day period, at some point, you may see the number going down. This does not mean you are losing money; it just means that the money that is missing is from more than 90 days before the day you are looking at it. That report has not been lost, though. There are other places you will see it, which you will learn further ahead.

Above the graphs, you can filter all of the results by marketplace, authors (in case you publish under multiple pen names), formats, title names, and date ranges. The date range is limited to the 90-day period, however, so for prior dates, you will need to check other reports on this page.

Below the royalties section, you will also see a button that says "Generate Report." By clicking that, you can download an Excel file in which you can see all of the information that is on this page. This is good if you are the kind of person who likes to keep a record of everything in a specifically organized way.

Historical

In the "Historical" tab, you will be able to see all of the sales that have been made ever since you published your first book. Here, you will see the exact same setup as the Sales Dashboard, except that you will see all of your sales instead of a specific time-range.

Just like with the Sales Dashboard, you can filter the results, and you can also generate a report that you can open as an Excel file. If you want to set a different date range, you can also do so. You are no longer limited to the 90-day period, but there are not many options to choose from either.

Month-to-Date

The "Month-to-Date" tab can be a useful section as well if you want more specific information. By default, you will see all of the sales of the current month for eBooks. This report will show the title of the book, the ASIN, the number of units sold, refunded, pages read, free units downloaded, and the number of books that were purchased while Amazon is matching your price to another website.

Just like with previous reports, you can filter this one, but there are fewer filters. You can filter it by marketplace, date range, and format. For the date range, you only have two options; current month, and previous month. For the formats, you can see either eBook or Paperback sales.

If you have several books and want to know which one is selling the most in the present or previous month, this is definitely the place to go. If you also want to know whether the eBook or the Paperback are selling more, you can find that out on this report as well.

Payments

Here, you will find the payments that have been made to you. There is a payment number, which is only good if you need to call KDP and ask about a specific payment. Then you will see the sales period, which will show the date range in which books were sold for this payment. Then the marketplace, the status, the date, the payment method (whether it was bank or check), the net earnings, exchange rate (for other marketplaces), and the amount of money that was paid to you.

To the left of each payment, there is a plus sign. You can click on it if you want additional information about the payments, although it really is not necessary. All it does it break down the payment with a little bit more detail.

At the bottom, you will find the "Generate Report" button as well. Just like with the first two reports, this will generate an Excel file so that you can view all of this information.

Pre-Orders

If you have created any pre-orders, you can view them here. If somebody purchases a pre-order book, it will not appear in the Sales Dashboard because you will not be paid until after the book has been released, so here you will see how many people have pre-ordered it.

Promotions

If your eBook is enrolled into KDP Select, you can create a free book promotion or a Countdown Deal. In this section, you can see the marketplace where your promotions were made, the ASIN, title, start time, end time, and status.

You will not see any information about the sales during the promotions here, since that can be seen in the other reports. This section is mostly to keep track of how many promotions you have created, and for which books.

Prior Months' Royalties

In this report, you will see the royalties earned for every specific month ever since you published your first book. Here, you will not see any specific information like the title nor the ASIN of the book; you will only see the amount of money per marketplace.

The only filter you will find is for the month that you want to view. Below that, you will see the amount of money you made for each marketplace, and you will see the amount for eBooks, Paperbacks, pages read, and the total.

If you are looking at the current month, you may be shocked to see that the "Total Royalty" section says "N/A." Do not worry about that, though, since it is normal. It will only show the total once the month is over. All other months that you look at will certainly have a number here, even if that number is zero.

Ad Campaigns

This tab used to have more information on it than what it shows now, but since ad campaigns have changed so much since they were first launched, this tab is different from what it used to be. You used to be able to access your campaigns dashboard, but now you will only see a link to the help page. Click on it, and you will see the links to the different ad campaigns marketplaces.

If you already have campaigns, or if you have already accessed this dashboard in the past, you will have no problem with this part. However, if this is your first time with ads, these links may not work for you. In a chapter further ahead, you will learn how to access these pages and create your ads.

Tax Forms

Although there are no reports for tax information on this page, it is also a topic that should be taken into consideration here. Once a year, KDP will send you tax forms so that you can report your sales to the IRS.

In order to access these forms, you can go directly to Tax Central, which is a page that controls all tax forms for any type of Amazon website you may use to make money in different ways. To get there, you should visit taxcentral.amazon.com and sign in with your Amazon e-mail address and password.

Once you have logged into your account, you will see a button near the bottom that says "Find Forms." Click on that, and you will see any tax forms you may have separated by year. Click on the one that you want, and you will be able to download your tax form.

The document you will open here is not for you to just send to the IRS; it is only to provide all of the information that you will need when reporting to the IRS.

Just remember that no matter which country you live in, if you are making money on a website like KDP that is based in the USA, you will need to report your earnings to the IRS. Not doing so can be dangerous, since just like any government tax organization, they want the money that is due to them.

If at any time you want guidance on how to report to the IRS, do not contact KDP; they are not experts on this topic, and they are not trained to handle these types of questions. For any guidance you may need, contact the IRS directly, or get in touch with a tax adviser.

The Detail Page

With your book published and live, you may think that there is nothing else to do but just sit back, relax, and wait for the money to come in. You would be wrong. The truth is, there are so many more aspects to take into consideration to make your book much better, and in this chapter, you will learn all about them.

Look Inside

The Look Inside feature is of utmost importance, because this will give readers the chance to take a look at a sample of your book to see whether they like it or not. With so many books on Amazon, it is not easy for an author to sell books unless they are already famous. If you are reading this book, chances are that you are not just yet, so you will need to take advantage of this feature.

Surprisingly, there are authors who decide to opt out of Look Inside claiming that they do not want anyone to read any part of the book for free. As a reader myself, if I see a book without it, I will not take the chance, so just imagine how many other readers may feel the same way.

Now once your book is published, you may feel a little anxious for the Look Inside feature to show up immediately, but you will have to be a little patient; it normally takes up to seven days for it to be activated (or less), but it can even take up to ten days, so if that timeframe has not gone by, do not bother the folks at KDP, because they will not be able to speed up the process.

Since the formats are different, Look Inside works differently for eBooks and Paperbacks. For example, for a Paperback book, you will see each page the way it will look when it is printed. For an eBook, unless you have a fixed format, there will not be any page breaks, and that is normal.

Another difference is the percentage that can be viewed. For eBooks, the default is 10%, while the Paperbacks will show 20% as default. You can request for this to be changed at any time (unless your book is erotica). Just contact KDP and let them know how much you want to show.

Do not bother requesting specific pages, though, since the system automatically chooses which pages will show. The only thing you can request is to change the percentage. For eBook, you can request anywhere between 5% and 45%, as long as the number is divisible by five. For example, you will not be able to request 27%; you can choose 25% or 30%, but nothing in the middle.

For Paperback books, you can choose anywhere between 10% and 80%, as long as the number is divisible by ten. For either of the two editions, if the Look Inside feature even shows any spoilers, contact KDP and they can remove them. If there are no spoilers, though, they cannot remove the pages.

If at any time you decide that you do not want to show a sample of your book, just contact KDP and request for the Look Inside feature to be removed. Just know that if you ever resubmit new files, this feature will reset, and regardless of any changes you may have requested, it will revert to default, and you will need to request the changes to be made again.

Keep in mind that Look Inside does not work on most mobile devices, so do not contact KDP to complain that you do not see it on your Amazon app. There is a way that the sample can be viewed on a mobile device, though, but it only works for eBooks. On the right, where you see the option to purchase the book, below all of the buttons, you will see a "Share" option. Choose either of the options there, and you can share a sample that can be viewed on any device that has access to the internet.

Thumbnails

Once the Look Inside feature is fully active, you will see two small thumbnail images below the main front cover image, which are the front and back cover images. There may be times in which you will want to show more than that, even without having to access the Look Inside feature. For example, if you have a map, you may want the map to show as one of the thumbnails.

If this is the case, do not contact KDP about this, because they will not be able to help you out. Unfortunately, KDP does not have the option to add extra thumbnail images, but there is another option, which is called Seller Central.

Seller Central is an Amazon website in which you can sell items on Amazon as a third-party seller. With the method you are about to read about, you do not actually have to become a seller; you only need to use the website to add the images and nothing more. If you are interested in becoming a seller, though, you can read my other book, "Selling on Amazon: A Step-by-Step Guide to Using Amazon's Seller Platform," in which you will learn everything you need to know for that website as well.

To add the thumbnails to your book, the first thing you will need to do is to create a seller account at services.amazon.com. You will see a big button that says "Register Now." Ignore that button and scroll down until you find an option that says "Sign up to become an individual seller." That way you will not have to pay a monthly fee for this account.

Once you have finished registering your account, you will see several options at the top. The second one says "Inventory." Hover the cursor over that and click the "Add a Product" option. Near the bottom, you will see a search bar; enter the ISBN of your book or the ASIN (which is the same as the ten-digit ISBN) and click "Search." You will see the book there, and the option to sell yours.

Now fill out all of the information that is requested, and if you do not want to sell your book yourself, enter a zero in the "Quantity" field. Once your done, you can go ahead and complete the process by clicking "Save and finish." It can take up to an hour for it to show correctly on your inventory, but usually it takes less time.

Make sure you are on your inventory page by clicking "Inventory" at the top, and once your book is there, you will see a button on the far right with two arrows; one pointing up, and the other pointing down. Click on that button, and choose the "Manages Images" button.

Here, you will be able to upload new images and then save the changes. Once you have done so, do not think that they will show up immediately; you actually have to contact Seller Support and request for them to update it. They may ask for proof that the image actually correspond to the book.

To contact Seller Support, just click "Help" on the top-right corner and select the "Get Support" option. There you will choose the reason why you are contacting, and depending on which options you choose, you may only be able to send an e-mail, or you may also be able to contact them by phone.

Categories

Categories are necessary for your book to be ranked properly. When you were setting up your book, you had the option to add two categories to your book, but you can actually have up to ten assigned to each book. You will not be able to add them yourself though; instead, you will need to contact KDP.

Before contacting, though, you need to know exactly which categories you want, and you need to provide the full category path. For example, if your book is about elves, do not just say that you want your book added to the "Elves" category because on one hand, that category may or may not exist, and on the second hand, if it does, there may be several different category paths that end in "Elves," so you need to specify which one you want.

There are different category paths depending on what type of book you are requesting categories for. If it is a Paperback, the path will start with "Books." You cannot add any paths like this to an eBook. For eBooks, the path will start out with "Kindle Store." These paths cannot be added to Paperback books. Ahead you will see two examples:

Kindle Store > Kindle Books > Business & Investing > Reference > Writing
Books > Sports & Outdoors > Outdoor Recreation

To find the correct paths, you must go to Amazon.com first of all. There, you may see an option that says "Departments" under the search bar, or you may see a button with three lines on the top-left corner. Whichever one you see, it will have a menu in which you will find both the "Books" and the "Kindle" options.

Select the one you need, depending on which edition you want to select the categories for, and you will be taken to a category page. There, you will see on the left column that there is a section that says "Kindle Store," and below that "Kindle ebooks" (for ebooks) or just "Books" and then a list of subcategories starting with "Arts & Photography" (for paperbacks). Below "Kindle ebooks" or "Books" is a list of categories. So following the first example above, if you were to click "Business & Investing," you would see more sub-categories. You would then click on "Reference," and then "Writing." That would be one full category path.

Contact KDP and send the list of categories you want, and they will be able to add them for you. Do not make the mistake of sending only the categories for one edition and ask the add the equivalents to the other edition, because it does not work that way. If you want categories on both the eBook and the Paperback, send the right categories for both.

Once the categories are added, it can take up to 72 hours for them to show on Amazon. One aspect you must take into consideration is that they will not all show on the detail page of your book. The whole purpose of categories is not for them to show on the detail page, but for the book to show up on the category page. On the detail page of your book, only the top three will be displayed.

Series Bundles

If your books are in a series, you may want them to be linked on a series page. If it is an eBook series, contact KDP and request for the series bundle to be created. As long as there are no pre-orders, customers will be able to purchase all books in the series with just one click.

If the series is in Paperback format, you will have to contact Author Central for that. They will not create a series bundle to purchase with one click, but they create a series page in which customers can see all the books in that series. If you do not have an Author Central account, just contact KDP and they will transfer the request to Author Central.

To link your book as a series, there are some requirements that must be met. This was already mentioned earlier in this book, but I will repeat them here as well.

If the books are in a series, then the series must have its own title. For example, one of the books I have written is called "The Wrath of Glothier," but it is part of a series called "The Daguco Chronicles." Each book in the series must have the same series title. When creating the book, there is an option for the book title and another one for the series title. If the series title does not match for all books, the series bundle cannot be changed.

Each book must also have a volume number, and the books should have a logical order. There are series that do not have a logical order; for example, cookbooks can be part of a series (not in the traditional sense), but since they are just cookbooks, they can be read in any order the reader wants. These types of series are not eligible for a series bundle.

Each volume number must be a whole number. For example, if you add volume 1.5, it will not be eligible. The number also has to be higher than zero; if you create a prequel and add volume number zero, the series will not be eligible for a bundle.

Moreover, the volume number of each book should not only be on the details that you added on KDP; it should also show somewhere else. If you can put the number on the cover of the book or one of the first pages, that would be best. If you do not want it there, though, at least add it to the description.

If your series is made up of books from different authors, KDP will have to contact each of the authors to request permission to add their books to your series. Before contacting KDP, contact the authors and let them know that they will also be contacted about this, so they will need to respond before the page is created.

Once you have submitted your request, it can take up to a week (in most cases) for them to process your request. Once they do, they will send you a link with the series page, so you can provide that to customers if you want. Furthermore, when you look at any of these books on Amazon, you will see a banner that shows that the book is part of a series, and by clicking on that banner, you will see the series page in order to see the rest of the books.

Detail Page Linking

If you have multiple editions of the same book, you may want to have them linked on the detail page, so that customers can see one book and automatically select the other without having to search for it. This is called linking, and if all information matches on the different editions, they should link automatically within three to five days. If not, you can contact KDP.

As mentioned above, all information must match, and I stress that point because if even the subtitle or author name are slightly different, even if you contact KDP, they will not be able to link the books for you.

The information that must match is the following:

> ➢ Title
> ➢ Subtitle
> ➢ Author Name
> ➢ Volume Number
> ➢ Edition Number (only applies to non-fiction)

If any of the above does not match exactly, then you can change it on the eBook, since you cannot change this metadata for a Paperback once it has been published.

Sometimes authors will contact KDP and say that they do not care about linking the books; they just want the reviews to be linked. Well let me tell you that the only way to link reviews is the link the books, so if the above data does not match, it cannot and will not be done, so you will need to make sure it is identical.

Once you contact them and they send you the response that they are linked, it normally takes just a few hours before you see the two editions linked on the detail page, although it can take up to 48 hours. If you do not see them linked, clear cookies and cache on your browser, and you will see it. After that, it can take up to five days for the reviews to be linked, and within those five days, you may even see the reviews disappear, but do not freak out, since this is only temporary; they will return shortly.

Other Marketplaces

Digital content can be very tricky in other marketplaces. When I say other marketplaces, I am referring to Amazon.co.uk, Amazon.de, and other countries that have their own Amazon page. With digital content, you will only be able to view it properly on your own marketplace, which means that if you are located within the US, you will only see your eBook properly on Amazon.com.

If you try to view your eBook on any other marketplaces, you may see that it says that the content is not available. In most cases, if you sign out, you will see it showing available for purchase.

Another issue that could arise is with the price. If you have different prices on different marketplaces, then you may see the wrong price when visiting those other marketplaces. Because it is digital content, it will show you the equivalent of the price on your home marketplace. Again, signing out should solve this issue.

If even after signing out you are not able to view the book they way it should look, contact KDP. If there is actually a problem with that marketplace, they will be able to investigate. If there is no problem, they will send you a screenshot so that you can confirm that everything is alright.

Customer Reviews

No matter how good your book is, chances are that at some point, you will receive a negative review. In most cases, this is not such a bad thing; if you see any item that has 100% five-star reviews, you may become skeptical about that item and think that the reviews are fake.

There may be reviews, however, that are not just negative, but inappropriate. For example, if they personally attack you as an author, or if they are about a totally different book, then you may want to have the review removed.

Keep in mind that whether the review says "Verified Purchase" or not, it will be considered a valid review. Since most items can be purchased on other websites and in physical stores, a customer can review an item even if they did not purchase it on Amazon, and that is fine. The only way they will not be able to leave a valid review is if they have not made enough purchases on Amazon that year.

If you find a review that you do not like, you can request to have it removed. Just take into account that KDP cannot do absolutely anything about these reviews, so even if you call and yell, they will not be able to help you directly. What they will do is to send your request to the communities team which will evaluate whether the review can be removed or not.

If you do not receive the response you expected, you can reply directly to the e-mail with said response. This team does not have any type of phone support, so your only way of talking to this team is through e-mail.

In the end, they will have the final word. If the review does not break any of the regulations, it will stay where it is, no matter how bad it makes your book look. The best that you can hope for is for other people to read your book and leave good reviews.

You may be tempted to leave a review yourself or ask a family member to do so. If Amazon detects that this is happening, they will not allow the review to go through. Also, if someone you know left a review and it did not go live, it could be that their account is not active enough for them to be eligible to leave reviews.

KDP Select

As mentioned previously in this book, KDP Select is an exclusivity program that only applies to eBooks. If you want your eBook to be enrolled in KDP Select, you can still sell your Paperback anywhere else you want, but the eBook itself must only be sold through KDP. With the book enrolled into this program, it will be in the Kindle Unlimited program, and you will also be able to schedule free book promotions and Countdown Deals.

Enrollment

If you did not enroll your book initially, you can do so at any time later on. On your bookshelf, you will see a button to the far right of your eBook that says "Promote and Advertise." Click on that button, and you will see an option to enroll.

Once your book is enrolled, it will last 90 days. By default, the enrollment will be automatically renewed. If you do not want that to happen, in the same place where you saw the enrollment button, there will be another one that says "Manage KDP Select Enrollment." There you can turn off that setting.

After enrolling the book, if you ever want to cancel the

enrollment without having to wait for the 90-day period to end, you can certainly do so. On the enrollment settings, you will have the option to cancel the enrollment in the first days. If you do not see this option, just contact KDP and they will cancel the enrollment for you at any time.

Keep in mind that Public Domain books are not eligible for KDP Select. The reason behind this is simple; a Public Domain book will never be exclusive to KDP, since it is totally free material, and anybody could publish it anywhere else as well. If your book is not eligible for this program, KDPs system will detect it, and you will not see the option to enroll your book. If you believe that your book is eligible and you do not see the option, contact KDP.

Kindle Unlimited

There are many readers who are subscribed to the Kindle Unlimited program, and in many cases, they will only read books that are in this program. If your book is not in this program, those are potential readers that you may miss out on. The question you must ask yourself, though, is if it is worth it to you for those readers to have access to your book through Kindle Unlimited.

In this program, readers can take any book and read it for free, and then they have to return it in order to read another book. It is very similar to a library, since they do not keep any of the books. This may be a deal breaker for you if you do not want anyone to read your book for free. You will be paid, though, so that is something to keep in mind.

Do not expect to receive the same amount of royalties as when you book is sold. It all depends on how many pages were read, and how much money Amazon made with Kindle Unlimited that month. In most cases, you will only make a few cents off of each book read. There could still be some benefit from this, though, since those customers could possibly leave a review on your book.

It is totally up to you whether you want your book to be in this program or not. It has its pros and cons, so put it all in the balance and decide whether you want Kindle Unlimited members to read your book for free or not.

Free Book Promotion

A free book promotion can be very helpful to obtain reviews and make yourself known. In many cases, authors will create these types of promotions regularly for the first book in a series so that the readers will become hooked and then purchase the other books.

For each 90-day enrollment period, you have the right to make your book for free for five days. They can be consecutive, or they can be separate; it is all up to you. If you have created a Countdown Deal during this period, though, you will not be able to create a free book promotion.

To create this promotion, click on the "Promote and Advertise" button to the far right of your eBook. On the left-hand side, you will see a section that says "Run a Price Promotion." Under that, you will see the options for the Countdown Deal and for the free book promotion. Select the latter and click the "Create a New Free Book Promotion" button.

You will see an option to select the start date, and another one for the end date. Select the dates there and click "Save Changes." If you do not want the days to be consecutive, you will have to create more than one free book promotion with the specific days you want the book to be free.

Once the day comes, your book will be free for people to download. Keep in mind that it will start at midnight Pacific time. If you do not see that it is free yet, clear cookies and cache.

Remember that while there is a free promotion active, you will not receive any royalties for books downloaded for free. Moreover, the sales rank will be totally different; there will be a free sales rank, and once the book has a price again, it will revert to the normal sales rank, which will have a different number.

I understand this could be a bit frustrating and even confusing, but there is logic behind this; a book that has a price on it cannot compete so well against a free book, so that is why Amazon will always separate the sales rank for books that have a price and books that can be downloaded for free.

Kindle Countdown Deals

Countdown Deals can be helpful since there is a lot of visibility of the discount on Amazon. When a Countdown Deal is active, the original price will show up with a slash on it, and the discounted price will be underneath it. There will also be a timer that indicates how long before the price will go up.

Another benefit is that for customers who already know how Amazon works, they can search Google for Countdown Deals, and this will direct them to a page on Amazon in which all books with this promotion will show up, giving your book more visibility.

For each 90-day enrollment period, you can set one Countdown Deal per book. However, if you have already used a free promotion day for that book, you will have to wait until the next enrollment period starts in order to create the discount.

To create this promotions, click on the "Promote and Advertise" button to the far right of your eBook. On the left-hand side, you will see a sections that says "Run a Price Promotion." Under that, you will see the options for the Countdown Deal and the free book promotion. Make sure that the former is selected, and click the "Create a New Kindle Countdown Deal" button.

The settings here are more complex than with a free book promotion since there are more options. First, you will have to select the marketplace where you want the discount. For now, only Amazon.com and Amazon.co.uk are available.

The next options you will see are for the start date and end date. You can run the promotion for up to seven days. Then, you will see the option for the number of increments. The options you see here depend on the original price of your book. For example, if your book is only $2.99, you will only have two increments if you choose the lowest discount price.

The last option is to choose the starting price. The lowest is 99 cents. Following the previous example, if your book is $2.99, and if you choose two increments, then the price will begin at 99 cents, and there will be a timer letting customers now when it will be priced at $1.99. After that, the timer will show for $2.99, until it reaches the original price.

Keep in mind that if you do not have the option to create a Kindle Countdown Deal and you have not run any free book promotions, it could be because you have recently changed the price, or the book has not been enrolled in KDP Select for more than 30 days. You cannot change the price of your book within 30 before the Countdown Deal nor 14 days after.

Ad Campaigns

If you want your book to sell, you will have to market it; do not think that just because it is live on Amazon, people will find it and buy it. There are most likely many other books that have similar keywords as yours, and because of that, when a customer searches for a book, they will likely find others that have had more sales and reviews. The solution is marketing.

The good news is that KDP has its own marketing service, and you can set your own budget. However, before I get into that, keep in mind that you can also do free marketing on your own, because not everyone purchases on Amazon.

The most common way people market books is on social media. For example, Facebook has many groups for different types of interests. Look for readers' groups and post your book there. Go to Goodreads and use that site for marketing. Even perform a Google search for free marketing. You will find a lot of information about different strategies so that you can decide which is best for you.

On KDP, you will find two different types of marketing services (Ad Campaigns). One is called Sponsored Products, and the other is called Lockscreen Ads. Ahead you will learn how to work with both of them. First though, it is important to learn how to get to the advertising platform.

For the very first time, you will need to go to your Bookshelf. If you want to work with an eBook, you will see a button on the far-right that says "Promote and Advertise." If it is for the Paperback, you will need to open the three-dots button menu and click the option with the same name.

You will see a section that says "Run an Ad Campaign." There, you will see a drop-down menu that says "Choose a marketplace." For now, you only have three options, which are Amazon.com, Amazon.co.uk, and Amazon.de. That is more than what we had before, since previously, you could only create a campaign for Amazon.com. Choose the marketplace you want and click the "Create and ad campaign" button.

After you have done this for the first time, whenever you want to go back, just visit advertising.amazon.com. Click the "Sign in" button on the top-right, and choose the "Advertising console (formerly Amazon Marketing Services)" option.

You will now see the two aforementioned ad campaigns. Select one, and you may be prompted to enter payment information. Do that, and you will be able to create your campaigns.

Sponsored Products

Sponsored Products is the most common ad campaign since it is versatile in every aspect. You can create this campaign for either eBook or Paperback, or you can create one for each. Moreover, customers will see it on whichever device they are using.

The way this works is that when customers type in specific keywords, there is a chance that your book will show up at the top. You do not pay anything for the book to show up; you only pay when somebody clicks on the book. You may be wondering how much you pay. Well, this depends on you, which you will learn about further ahead.

Also, if a customer is looking at a book that is similar to yours, there is a possibility that your book will show up as a sponsored product on that detail page. This will add more chances of customers finding your book and possibly purchasing it.

Once you select this option, you will have to enter the requested information for your ad. First, you will need to enter a campaign name. I recommend entering the name of the type of edition into the campaign name; for example, for the book, I would set the name "Self-Publishing on KDP Paperback," or "Self Publishing on KDP eBook" so that it will be easier to track them.

Next, you will have to enter a start date. If you want the campaign to last a specific amount of time, you can set an end date. If you want it to be indefinite, leave that section empty. You can stop a campaign at any time.

Now you will have to set a daily budget. This can be anywhere between $1 and $1 million. Your budget will ensure that you will not pay more than you can each day. As an example, if you were to set a daily budget of $1, then it will be possible to spend less than a dollar (depending on how many clicks you get), but you will not spend more. The budget is your limit.

How much you pay per click depends on you. At this point, you will not determine the exact price per click yet, but you will further ahead. To understand budgets (and other sections) better, though, you do need to know how this system works.

You will be able to set a bid. When a customer types in one of your campaign keywords, there is a chance that your book will show up. If someone else has an ad campaign with the same keyword and has a higher bid than you do, then their book will show up. If your bid is higher, then your book will show up. If a customer clicks on your book, you will pay whatever the bid is.

For the next section, you will determine which keywords will be used for this campaign. You can select manual targeting, in which you can set your own keywords, or you can select automatic targeting, in which the system will automatically determine which keywords will generate this ad.

Unless you have a marketing expert or know how to search for the best terms to use for keywords, your best book could possibly be to select automatic targeting. The choice is yours, though. Some people recommend creating two separate ads so that one can have manual and the other can use the automatic, and that way you can see which does better.

In the following section, you can choose a bidding strategy. When you are almost done, you will be able to select your bid, but this section determines the behavior of said bid. You can select dynamic bids, in which there is a chance for the bid to go higher and lower, thus paying more or less. If you do not want to pay more than what you set, you can choose the one that only makes it go lower.

You can also choose the "Fixed bids" option. That way, your bid will always remain the same, and you will never pay any more nor any less. Below that, you can even adjust bids. If you want the search results bids to be higher, or if you want the sponsored products on other detail page bids to be higher, adjust a percentage here.

The next step is to select the ad format. If you want a custom text to show up on the ad, select "Custom text ad." You will only be able to promote one book per ad, though. If you want to promote multiple books with the same ad, choose "Standard ad," but you will not be able to add a custom text.

Now you can select which book(s) to add to this ad campaign. You can either scroll down the list or type the name of your book or ASIN in the text box. Once you found the book you want, click on the "Add" button to the right.

If you chose automatic targeting, in next section you will set a general bid; in other words, how much you will pay per click. If you chose manual targeting, you will have to enter keywords, click the "Add keywords" button, and then set an individual bid for each of the keywords that you entered.

You also have the option of entering negative keywords. This means that any time a customer searches for any of these keywords, Amazon will not show your book. This is optional, so you can just leave it blank if you do not want any negative keywords.

Instead of targeting by keywords, you can also target by categories. Right above where you see the space to enter the keywords, select "Product Targeting" so that you will be given the option to select categories that you want your book to show up with. Also, instead of categories, you could select specific products for your book to show up with, but that is not so commonly used.

If you selected the "Custom text ad," you will now be able to enter the text that you want customers to see when your ad shows up. You can only write up to 150 characters, so keep it short and simple. You will also be able to see how your ad will look.

Once you are done, you are now able to complete the process. Click on the "Launch campaign" button, and it will be submitted for review. After the review is complete, you will receive an e-mail letting you know whether it was approved or not. If your book is not in English, or if it is an erotica book, the campaign may be rejected.

Lockscreen Ads

Lockscreen Ads can also be useful, but they are not so versatile, since they only apply to eBooks, and the minimum budget is much higher. The way it works is that when a customer is using a Kindle device, they will see ads on the lockscreen, and this program can give you a chance of showing yours there.

Once you select this option, you will be asked to create a campaign name, just like with the Sponsored Products. After that, you will need to set a start date and end date. Unlike with Sponsored Products, these campaigns cannot run indefinitely; the limit is six months. You can end it at any time, though.

Next, you will set a lifetime budget. This is the limit of money for the entirety of the campaign. That means that if you use up the whole budget after a few weeks, the campaign will end. The minimum budget for this type of campaign is $100, and the maximum is $1 million. This may sound like a lot of money, but the next step can help you so that it does not hit too hard.

Now you will get to set the pacing. Do you want people to see your ad as quickly as possible even if it means burning through your budget in a short period of time? Or do you prefer it to be paced out so that you do not spend all that much money at once? You have those two options here, so choose wisely.

Once you have done that, you will get to select which book you want to show up on the ad. After finding the correct one, click the "Add" button. You can only select one book per campaign.

The next step is to select the categories. It is recommendable to select categories that are similar to the one your book is in, so that there will be more chances of the readers being interested in the book. Here, you will be able to select multiple categories.

Now you can set your bid. The minimum is $0.02, although that kind of bid might not get you very far. Once you have selected your bid, type in the text you want readers to see when your ad shows up. Again, the limit is 150 characters. You will then be able to preview it to see how it will look in a Kindle E-reader or Fire Tablet. Once you are done, click the "Submit for review" button.

Campaigns Dashboard

Now that you have created your campaigns, you will want to monitor them. When you first log into advertising.amazon.com, you will be able to see the number of impressions your campaigns have, clicks, sales, etc.. Just keep in mind that what you see in sales is not the amount of royalties you make, but the retail price.

There will be several metrics there to show you the progress of your campaigns, and you will also see an option that says "Add metric." Click on that if you want even more information. Also, by clicking on a specific campaign, you will see the same information, but only for that specific campaign.

If you have multiple books with different campaigns, you can also create portfolios. On the top-left, you will see the option that says "Create a Portfolio." That way you can place specific campaigns into the portfolios and track the information separately from the rest. It is totally optional, though.

To the left of each campaign name, you will see a switch. Click on that to terminate that specific ad campaign, and you can click it again to turn it back on.

If you hover your cursor over the button with three lines on the top-left, you will see a menu. There is an option there that says "Reports." Click on that, and you will be able to generate spreadsheet reports with all the information about each campaign.

Now that you have learned how to use campaigns, you can start testing it out and see what works the best for you. I cannot offer specific advice because each case is different, but you will be able to determine what is best for your books after a little experimentation.

Ordering Books

When it comes to Paperback books, there will be times in which you will want to order your own books. It may be so that you can have a copy to show off, or maybe you actually want to sell your own copies. Also, before publishing the book, you may want to order a proof to make sure it looks right. Whatever the reason may be, you will be able to order copies of your book, and you will pay only printing costs and whatever it takes to ship it to you (shipping and handling, taxes, etc.). In this chapter, you will learn how it is done.

Printed Proofs

Before you publish your book, it is highly recommended to order a proof copy. You may have already seen the Print Preview, and it may look great, but what you see on the monitor is not necessarily what will be printed out. If you do decide to order a proof copy, there are two ways to do it.

If you are setting up your book, on the pricing page you will see the option to order a printed proof right above the "Publish" button. Click on that, and you will be asked for the quantity and the marketplace. If you are in the US, select Amazon.com. For other countries, select the one that is closest to country where you live.

Click the "Submit Proof Request" button, and you will see a pop-up window letting you know that it can take up to four hours for the order to be ready to be placed. Click "Confirm Proof Request" and wait. Within four hours, you will receive an e-mail telling you that the proof copy is in your cart. Go to Amazon and click on the shopping cart and place your order.

If you have finished setting up your book and you are on the Bookshelf, you do not have to go to the pricing page to request your proof copy; you can do it right there from the Bookshelf. Hover your cursor over the three-dots button to the far-right of your book and select the "Request Printed Proofs" option. The rest is the same as mentioned above.

While you are on the shopping cart, on the last page, you will see an estimated delivery date. Once you have placed the order, you may receive it before that, but normally it should not take more. Once you receive the book, look through it. If you are satisfied, you can then publish the book. Just remember that even though it may look great to you, if it does not meet the requirements, it will not pass the review process no matter how many times you call KDP.

These printed proofs will be just like the normal retail copy of your book in almost every aspect. There are two differences, though. On one hand, printed proofs have a band at the top that says "Not for resale." Basically, this is to make sure that if your book does not meet certain quality standards, people cannot blame Amazon, since KDP did not approve that book yet.

The other difference is in the barcode. Instead of showing the ISBN, it will show a custom barcode specific to that particular order, and it will have a ten-digit ASIN (Amazon identifier) underneath it.

You can order up to five copies at a time. If that is not enough, you will have to place several different orders. You may wonder why anybody would need more than one. There is a simple reason, though; it is so that multiple people can proof your book. For example, if you have an editor or an illustrator, they can make sure it looks good too.

Another reason to order additional copies is for Beta readers. Basically, a Beta reader is someone who will read your book and provide feedback. You could just send them the book digitally, but not everyone likes to read from a screen, so this could be a viable option for you if that is the case.

Author Copies

With the book live and available for purchase, you will also be able to order author copies. The only difference between an author copy and a retail copy that customers buy on Amazon is the price; it is the same exact book in every other way. If you want to order your book, go ahead and do so at any time.

To order author copies, the process is very similar to that of ordering proof copies, except faster. On your Bookshelf, you will see a button on the far-right of your book that says "Order Author Copies." It should be to the left of the three-dots button. If your book has any unpublished changes, this button may say "Continue Setup." If that is the case, hover the cursor over the three-dots button, and you will see the option there.

Click the "Order Author Copies" option, and once again, you will see the options to select the quantity and the marketplace. You can order anywhere between one book and 999. Regardless of the quantity, you will always pay the same per book; there is no bulk discount because you are already getting the bulk discount even if you order just one. You are always paying the very minimum.

Enter your quantity and select the marketplace, and click "Submit Order." This will take you to your Amazon shopping cart, where you will have to complete your order. If you have a Prime membership, it will not work here, because this is not an Amazon order per se; it is a KDP order, and Prime does not apply here. No matter what, you will not get free shipping.

Just like with the printed proofs, once you are on the last page, you will see the expected delivery date. It is possible that it can be delivered before that, but there is no guarantee. Do not call KDP and ask them to get it to you faster, because they do not have the ability to do that.

Order Timelines

When ordering author copies, you may notice that the expected delivery date seems a bit far away. Interestingly, a customer ordering the book from Amazon will actually receive it faster than you will receive your author copy. Do not get upset over this, since it is normal, and it even makes sense.

When a customer buys your book, Amazon is printing that book and shipping it to the customer. Amazon does not print bulk orders usually, so it is fairly easy to print one or two books, ship them out, and get them delivered quickly.

On the other hand, when you order an author copy, KDP is the one that does the fulfillment. Since KDP prints thousands of books a day, you cannot expect them to ship your order out as quickly as Amazon will. If you have a book signing event or any type of time-sensitive need, be sure to place your order with enough anticipation to make sure you will receive it on time.

Most of the time, it will take around five days for KDP to print and ship your order. Once they have shipped it, the time it takes for it to be delivered depends on the shipping speed you chose. Available shipping speeds depend on where you are located. For example, in the US, you will have Standard Shipping (3 – 5 business days), Expedited Shipping (two business days), and Priority Shipping (one business day). If you placed the order with Standard Shipping, KDP will print the book and ship it, and then it will take up to five days for it to be delivered.

There are people who mistakenly think that if they choose Priority Shipping, since it is one-day shipping, they will receive it the very next day. That is certainly not how it works. It will take the normal time to print the book, and once they ship it, you will receive it the next day. If you are wondering why it would be worth it to pay a faster shipping speed, you will need to take into account that when you select a specific shipping speed, it will tell you when to expect it. If that date is not good for you, that is when it is worth it to select a different shipping speed.

Remember that when you are placing the order, you will always see the expected delivery date. The moment in which you click the "Place your order" button, you are agreeing to that date, so you do not really have any right to complain if you do not receive it earlier.

At some time, you may notice that it is taking more than five days for KDP to ship your book out. As mentioned previously, it takes this number of days most of the time, which means not always. Before you decide to complain, just remember that KDP is not promising to ship it within a certain timeline, but they are promising to deliver it within a certain timeline. If that date has not gone by, then nothing wrong has happened

If for some reason there has been a delay and you do not receive your order on time, just contact KDP and request compensation. They will not be able to provide a full refund since you will receive the books, but they can refund the shipping costs. No matter what, though, KDP will not have the power to speed up the process.

Order Troubleshooting

When placing your order, there are some scenarios you could come across that could impede your ability to place the order. In this section, you will learn how to solve them if you were to encounter any of them.

Empty Cart

Once you submit your order on KDP and you are taken to Amazon, you should see the books in your cart. However, there can be times in which you do not see any. Nine times out of ten, this will be because you are not signed into your account. If you are the unlucky number one in which this is not the case, contact KDP.

Most of the time, this issue occurs when using a foreign

marketplace. If you normally order items on Amazon.com, but you are sending a book to someone in Europe, chances are that you are not signed into any European Amazon account, so when you are redirected to Amazon, the cart will be empty just because of not being signed in.

If this is the case, just sign in, and you should see the books in your cart. If you are on your home marketplace and you still do not see anything in your book, it could still be that you are not signed into the correct account. Just sign out of Amazon and sign into the same account that is associated to KDP.

If you like to have your personal buyer account separate from your KDP account, just know that to order books from KDP, you will need to use the Amazon account associated to the same e-mail address as the KDP account. The system is not going to send the books to a different account.

Quantity Limit

Another issue you may encounter is a message saying that the seller only has a specific number of copies in stock, and if that is the case, it would seem that it will not allow you to order any number of copies higher than that. There is a solution, though.

At this point, you may be wondering, "How can there be a specific number in stock if this is print-on-demand?" Believe it or not, this is possible. If you order books at some point and then cancel the order before it was shipped out, there is a chance that they were already printed, and KDP is not going to just throw them away. These books will be sold in the next orders, and that is what causes this error message. This is only one example, as there are other ways in which there could be physical stock of your book.

If you do get this message and you want to order more than what it is allowing you to do, as I mentioned, there is a solution, so do not panic. Click the "Proceed to Checkout" button, and continue with your order as if there were not issues at all. On the last page where you have the option to place the order, you will also see the quantity on the bottom of the page. You will have the option to change that quantity; do so, and click the "Update" button, and your order will be updated successfully.

Be careful with this method, because in the shopping cart, there are two sections in which you can change the quantity; one is on the first page of the cart, and the other is on the last page, where you place the order. This method will only work on the last page.

Old Edition Received

If you every update the manuscript of your book, you will expect to receive the most updated edition. If this is the case, there could be two reasons: physical stock, or unpublished changes.

The first thing you will need to do is check your book out in your Bookshelf. If it shows as just "Live," Then the newest manuscript should be the one that KDP should print. If it is showing as "Live with unpublished changes," chances are that you uploaded the new manuscript, but you never actually published the change, or you tried to publish the change, but it was rejected.

In the latter case, KDP does not have any responsibility since it is actually not their fault. Before placing the order, you should verify that the book is fully live with no unpublished changes. If you did not do so, then KDP cannot be held accountable for this error.

If the book is fully live and you still received the wrong edition, it could be because there was physical stock of the old edition. If that is the case, just contact KDP and they will refund the book for you. If the issue persists even though there is no physical stock, again, contact KDP and request for them to investigate the matter.

Defective Copies

Since KDP is a print-on-demand company, there is always a possibility of defect. This does not mean that it is a bad company, because the same can happen with any other self-publishing website. If this occurs, contact KDP.

Keep in mind that some defects are not KDPs fault; it could be due to an issue with the file that you uploaded. For example, if you uploaded a cover file that looks great on the screen, but the printed version looks dark, it could be that the cover you uploaded does not have such a great quality.

Whatever may be the case, KDP will investigate, and if the error is on their side, they will solve the issue. If the error is on your side, they will explain how to solve it yourself.

There is a certain degree of variance that will not be considered a defect, though. For example, if your file has 0.5" margins, do not expect it to be exactly 0.5"; there will most certainly be a slight difference. Normally, this variance is not an issue. If it is, you may need to design your book a bit differently to allow for this variance, since it will not be considered a defect.

Customer Order Defects

Imagine this scenario: a friend of yours buys the book on Amazon, but when they receive it, there are defects. Although the chances of this happening are pretty low, it could happen. You may want to call KDP and demand an explanation and for compensation to be provided to the customer. That is not how it works, though.

Author orders and customer orders and handled separately, and because of that, KDP will not be able to help you out with a customer order. Anyway, since Amazon has security questions, nobody will be able to access the account where the order was placed unless the customer calls Amazon.

If this were to ever happen, the customer only needs to contact Amazon customer service. They will respond for this error, and it will not affect you in any way. Amazon can issue a refund for the order, and the customer can purchase it again to receive a correctly printed copy of the book.

You may be worried that the customer will not know that and will just get angry, but if that is the case, that is their own fault; if you receive a defective item and do not request compensation, nobody will ever be able to help you out.

If you are worried that you may receive a negative review for this, rest assured that in that case, there is a solution as well. Just write an e-mail mentioning the review and explaining that it is due to an Amazon manufacturing error, and KDP can forward that request to the team that can remove the customer review.

Author Central

You may have noticed that some books on Amazon have an author bio, editorial reviews, and even an author page. It is definitely recommendable that you have your own author page with its own bio, so here you will learn how to do that.

The first thing you need to know is that none of this is done on KDP. Remember, not all books are done through KDP, so in order to allow author pages for all books, it is done through a totally different website called Author Central.

Getting Started with Author Central

In order to start working on your Author Central account, you will need to visit authorcentral.amazon.com. Unlike with KDP, you will not be able to just sign in the first time; if you do so, you will just see a message saying that you do not have an Author Central account with that e-mail address.

Click the "Join Now" button, and you will be taken to the "Terms & Conditions" page. It is pretty short, so do yourself a favor and read it, and then click the "Accept" button.

You will then be asked to confirm your identity. It may show you some books and ask your if they are yours, or it may ask you to type in your name. Search for your book, and click "This is me." If you have not published yet, you will not be able to complete this process yet. Wait until you have a book that is live, and then come back.

Now that you have confirmed yourself, you will see a button that says "Go to Author Central." You will now be able to create your author page. You will see four tabs at the top: "Author Page," "Books," "Sales Info," and "Customer Reviews." Ahead, you will learn about each of these tabs and how to use them.

Author Page

The "Author Page" tab is essential for getting your page to look its best. Here, you can add your biography. It is best to write at least two paragraphs here about yourself, and do so in the third person. There are people who write it in first person, but it does not look so professional, so I do not recommend it.

If you are not sure what to write, look at the biographies of your favorite authors, and that can give you some ideas on how to do it. You can write what led you to become an author, some information about your personal life, talents, hobbies, etc. so that people can get to know the real you.

If you write under a pseudonym and prefer to remain anonymous, you do not need to tell so much about yourself. Just give enough information so that they can get to know a little bit about you, but not enough to give away your true identity.

Below the biography section, you will have the option to enter the RSS feed of your blog, if you have one. It is usually a good idea for authors to have blogs as it gives more visibility to yourself. Depending on which website you use to manage your blog, there will be different ways to get the RSS feed. If you are unsure about it, contact the website's support.

To the right, you will have the option to add a custom URL to your author page. This is very useful if you want to provide the link to someone and want it to be short. Just enter whatever you want there, and it will create your custom link.

Below that option, you will have the opportunity to upload your author photo. It should be either a JPEG, PNG, or GIF. Also, it should be between 300 to 8000 pixels in width and height, and it should be no bigger than 4MB. You can upload up to eight pictures. Once you upload them, it will go through a review process.

Next, you also have the option to upload videos. In most cases, these can be videos of book signings and any other events that you may participate in as an author. This is optional, though; if you do not want a video, you do not have to upload one.

Books

The fact that you created an author page does not mean that books will be added to it automatically. It could happen, but in most cases, you will have to add them manually. On the "Books" tab, you will see a button that says "Add more books." Click on that, and enter the ASIN, ISBN, title, or author name of your book and click "Go." Locate your book, and click the "This is my book" button.

It can take several days for the book to actually show up on your author page, so do not expect it to be there immediately. Now that it is there on your Author Central account, though, you can add more information to it. Just click on the title of the book, and you will see exactly what can be added.

Review

In most cases, you will have to pay for editorial reviews if you want them. There are many companies that offer them for a fee, so you can search for the right place that offers this service and request for a review. This is very different from a customer review, since it is done a review professionals.

If you have editorial reviews and you want to add them to your book, click "Add" here and place the review there. You should write either a sentence from the actual review or the whole editorial review followed by the name of the company or person who provided it. You will then be able to preview it to see how it will look, and then you can save the changes.

Description

You have the option to change the description here; however, it is not necessarily a good idea. If you make changes here, it will only reflect on one marketplace. Then, to change it on the others, you will have to go to the respective marketplaces to do so. For example, for the UK, you will need to visit authorcentral.amazon.co.uk and create an account there to add the description there as well.

If you want to make the change here anyway, you are free to do so; just click "Edit," and make the changes you want. You will then be able to preview your description, and then save the changes.

From the Author

Some books may have a "From the Author" section, which is basically a message from the author to the readers. This is totally optional; if you have something special you want to say to your readers, enter it here. If not, you can just leave this section blank.

If you want a "From the Author" section on your book and/or author page but you do not know what to write, I would suggest that you look for your favorite authors to see what they wrote. This could give you an idea of what you could enter here.

From the Inside Flap

If you only publish on KDP, you should leave this section blank, since KDP does not offer the option this option for your book. If you publish books with other companies that do allow you to have a flap with text on it, then you can enter the same text here if you want. If not, just leave it blank. Like the rest of the sections on this page, this is optional.

From the Back Cover

In many cases, the description on the detail page is the same as on the back cover. If that is not your case, then you can add the back cover text here so that people can read it directly on the detail page instead of having to click on the thumbnails.

If the description and back cover text are the same, then it is best to leave this section blank. If you add the same text, it will just be confusing and redundant, and that is something you definitely want to avoid at all costs.

About the Author

If you already entered a biography on the author page, it will automatically show up on the detail page of each book that is added to said author page. However, you have the option of entering a different "About the Author" text for each book individually if you want. If not, just leave this section blank.

Multiple Pen Names

If you write under different pen names, you will need a separate author profile for each one. With one profile already created, when you want to create a new one, you will do so on the "Books" tab. Following the process of adding a book, as soon as you try to add a book with a different author name, the system will detect this and ask you if you want to create a new profile. Follow this same process for as many pen names that you may have.

Author Central will allow you to have up to three different profiles on the same account. If you have more than that, you will need to create a new Amazon account and create the respective Author Central account so that you can add more profiles.

Just remember that for each profile, the books should have a matching author name. Avoid making any differences; for example, if you have a middle initial on your books, all books with that author name should have the middle initial, and so should the author profile. If not, there could be some issues, and even if you are able to add it to the profile, it will not look professional.

Sales Info

The "Sales Info" tab certainly has important information. However, you must be careful about how you interpret it; if you see a change here, it does not necessarily mean that you are entitled to additional royalties. For real-time information about your sales, you should always consult your royalty reports on KDP.

What you can find on this section is information on the sales rank of individual books and your author rank. This information depends not only on the number of sales you make, but also what other books in the same category make, which is why it is practically impossible to obtain specific date about how many sales were made.

You may be wondering what the point is, then. To put it simple, this is just so that you can compare your sales to other authors. Many people ignore this tab altogether, and I am certainly one of them. KDP offers the most accurate information you need.

If what you want is to track your sales rank due to a goal of becoming a best seller, then you can certainly come here to take a look (as opposed to opening each book on Amazon and checking the sales rank there), but this would only be informative, since there are no options here to change anything.

Customer Reviews

On this tab, you will see all of the customer reviews on each of the books on this author profile in one place. You will have all of the same options as if you were on the individual book's detail page; the only difference is that instead of going to each book's page one by one, you will see them all here.

You will see the name of the person who placed the review, the name of the book the review is assigned to, and then you can read the review itself. Below that, you will have the link to the Amazon page where the review is located. Then, you will have the option to add a comment, which is what any customer would have. Beside that, you will see another option that will take you to the link where all the reviews for that book are located.

Getting Help

If at any time you feel lost, click on the "Help" option on the top-right. There you will find many help pages that could possibly give you the information that you need. If that is not the case, you can contact Author Central directly by clicking on the "Contact Us" button on the left-hand side of the help section.

The page will give you a drop-down menu to select the reason why you are contacting. Select the closest one to your reason for contacting, and you will see more drop-down menus. Make the necessary selections until you see the option for e-mail and phone.

If the phone option is grayed out, that means that you are contacting outside of business hours, so you will either have to send an e-mail, or contact later. Author Central will usually answer e-mails within 24 hours. On weekends, they do not have phone support.

When dealing with Author Central agents, please treat them with respect; they want to help you out as much as possible, but if their answer is not to your likings, it does not mean that they are not doing their job, but that the policy is not necessarily what you want it to be. In the next chapter, you will learn about contacting KDP. Please apply the principles mentioned in that chapter to the Author Central agents, since the same information applies to them.

Contacting KDP

Although this book covers pretty much everything you will need to know about the Kindle Direct Publishing website, there may come a time in which you will need to contact them. If that is the case, rest assured that you can certainly do so, and they will be willing to help you out.

To contact them, you will need to click the "Help" option on the top-right of any KDP page. That will take you to the help section, and if you scroll down, you will see a "Contact Us" button on the left-hand side. Click on that, and you will be prompted to select the reason for contacting.

Click any of the options there, and most likely, a few more options will show up under that particular option. If that is the case, click on one of the new options, and you will see two options to the right, which will be E-mail or Phone.

If you do not see the phone option, send them an e-mail requesting to activate phone support, and they will do so. If by the time you are reading this you need to talk to them by phone right away, call Amazon.com customer service and request to be transferred to KDP. Once you are talking to one of the representatives, request that they activate phone support at once.

If the phone option is grayed out, it means that you are contacting outside of business hours. Unlike Author Central, KDP does offer phone support on weekends. You can either call back later or send an e-mail.

Keep in mind that KDP agents are there to help you, and there is no reason for them to refuse to help you out with something if it is in their power to do so. If you do not like their answer at any time, it is most likely because that is what their policies say. Never think that they are lying to you because that is not how they operate.

When KDP answers you, you will always receive an e-mail from them with a survey. This survey does not evaluate the internal policy; it evaluates the representative directly, so if that person treated you right, even if you did not like the answer, do not evaluate them negatively; it is not their fault.

Once you answer the first question (either yes or no), you will see a few questions in which you can rate the policy. If you are unsatisfied with KDP, you can vent out there instead of berating the agent or giving him a "No" on the survey.

If at any time you feel that the answer you received was not correct, you may feel tempted to evaluate the agent negatively. Before you do so, however, I would recommend that you call back. Ask the next agent if what the previous agent said was correct, and that way you will get a second opinion. If this agent confirms it, then do not give either one of them a negative evaluation.

If this agent tells you that the previous response is incorrect, then you can give the evaluation that you want. Know this, though: the person you are talking to is a human being, and as such, they are subject to mistakes in the same way you are. I am not saying that you should not evaluate negatively, but I do want you to take that into consideration when you contact KDP.

Of course, there will be times in which you may be frustrated; no company has policies that everyone will like. If that ever happens, just remember that when you are talking to someone on the phone, it is not that person's fault. Again, they are doing their best to help you out. If you yell at them, they are not going to help you more than if you talk calmly.

If you are especially rude on the phone, they might just hang up on you. This may seem harsh, but the truth is, nobody should have to deal with customers who insult the representatives that are trying to help, so they have all the right to do so.

Conclusion

As you have seen in this book, self-publishing on Amazon can be a great opportunity for you, but it is important to know how to do it. There is a lot of work to be done, but just the fact that you can do it all for free and have people help you out every step of the way is probably the biggest advantage of using KDP.

I hope you have learned a lot from this book. If that is the case, I am sure that you will be able to publish your book with no problem at all, and you can have the potential of making many sales.

Of course, there is more to learn about KDP, since writing everything would require a whole series of books instead of just one singe volume. However, if you have read the whole book, you will know how the website works, and you will be able to find the rest on your own.

I wish you the best of luck with your books! I hope to one day see your name on a list of best selling authors. If you follow all of my instructions and publish and market your book, that dream can certainly come true. Now, if you have not written your book yet, my question to you is, what are you waiting for?

If you enjoyed this book, show some support and write a customer review on Amazon. As a writer, you will certainly want reviews on your book, so show the same support that you would want to receive yourself.

Another book you may be interested in reading from the same
author:
Selling on Amazon: A Step-by-Step Guide to Using Amazon's
Seller Platform
By Paul Gutiérrez Covey